The Breastfeeding Handbook

The Essential Guide for New Mothers.
Simple and Quick Tips for Better and Confident
Breastfeeding, Lactation, and Weaning.

Table of Contents

Copyright © 2018

COPYRIGHT PROTECTION

Chapter 1. Getting Started: Preparing and the Basics of Breastfeeding

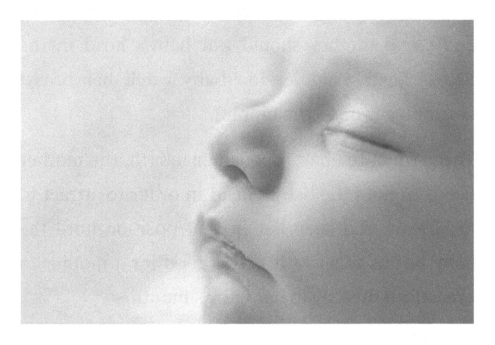

Although breastfeeding is the most natural way to nourish newborns, it is not just instinctive, it is a skill that is taught. Some mothers learn it spontaneously, so they start to enjoy breastfeeding their babies very quickly. Other women need time, help, encouragement, and support to breastfeed.

The baby's position during breastfeeding is very important. It is essential that a nursing mother takes a position where she feels relaxed and comfortable.

The baby should turn her body around the mother's body, and mother should put baby's head in the breast height and let the baby catch her breast (wrapping around the nipple).

Then, when the baby opens her mouth, the mother needs to hold the baby's head in order to attract to the breast and keep her in that position until the baby begins to suck. It is not good for a mother to breastfeed directly in her baby's mouth.

For nursing mothers who have problems with small nipples and have not successfully mastered the art of breastfeeding in the first few days, a silicone nipple can be helpful. In any case, if a mother is initially struggling with breastfeeding, she should seek professional help.

Although it sounds unlikely, some mothers have problems with over-producing milk, or producing milk when their babies are not feeding. This is especially the case in the first days after childbirth. For example, when thinking about a baby, when another baby cries, or in other situations that are suggestive of or similar to having a hungry baby.

It is often the case that while a baby feeds from one breast, milk appears from the other. The only "rescue" is the nursing inserts, which should be put into the bra. These are very practical, as they prevent clothes from dribbling and rescue mothers from unpleasant situations. This problem usually stops after the first month of breastfeeding.

If the baby is not sucking for a long time, for any reason, it is still necessary to maintain the secretion of milk. If it is necessary to stimulate the breasts and increase the amount of milk produced; it is also important to empty both breasts in order to increase the amount of milk in the pod.

The milk needs to be squeezed before breastfeeding if the breasts are tanned and the baby cannot "catch" the breast. This should be done even when the breasts are sore after breastfeeding, in order to prevent delay or other complications in the future.

Before weaning, a mother should consult a pediatrician. The type and quantity of milk adapted should be adapted to the baby's needs and age. Cow's milk is the worst choice as a replacement for mother's milk.

What determines the success of breastfeeding?

First of all, the key to successful breastfeeding is a mother's desire to breastfeed her baby, a positive emotional tune-up, and a belief that the beloved baby needs breast milk. Women who consciously chose to have a baby—and a long-awaited pregnancy—have shown to breastfeed longer.

Try not to pay attention to troubles, and put them aside for later. Nothing compares to the health of your child. Imagine the problems that you will encounter if you lose your baby breast milk, and those that you have now will definitely become less relevant.

The same logic applies to the father of the child: it depends on it largely on the moral (and material) well-being of the family, as well as the creation of a favorable environment for the natural feeding of his baby. The mother must be sure that she will be able to feed the baby with her milk. Quite often a caring father has already bought a mixture of artificial formula, "just in case," while the baby is still in the hospital. It would be very tempting to take advantage of it, especially when the baby is crying loudly. But be strong, both of you! As new parents, there will be many difficulties to face, but most of them can be overcome. You—mom—can overcome all!

Chapter 2. First Two Weeks after Childbirth (Problem-Solving During the First Week)

Breastfeeding is a natural way of feeding every newborn baby. Mother's milk is the best baby food, for many reasons. The female body is prepared to produce milk at the time of birth. Breast milk meets all of the baby's nutritional needs, and it adapts to the requirements of baby's growth.

In the first six months after birth, and especially during the first two weeks, breast milk is the only suitable baby food. After six months, it is necessary to enrich the diet with other foods, though breast milk should still be the basis of the baby's nutrition.

Mother's milk is not always the same; it changes during the baby maturation's, and even during the day.

Milk produced immediately after childbirth is known as colostrum. Colostrum contains more protein, and therefore more antibodies, than mature breast milk. It is especially important for newborn babies. In appearance, it is dense, sticky, and clear lukewarm liquid. Colostrum is the perfect first food for the newborn and contains more proteins and vitamin A than later milk. Even mothers with more than one child rarely have more than a few drops to a few milliliters of colostrum. The first serious quantities of milk begin to produce mainly on the second day after delivery.

In the first days after delivery, the production of breast milk is limited, but this fits the needs of newborn babies. Colostrum is rich in fat and proteins, which are very important for the future health of the baby.

Proteins are primarily immunoglobulins—carriers of "ready-made" antibodies to diseases that the mother was suffering from. Thus, they provide the newborn with protection from infectious agents that lurk in the outer environment. This is the first natural "vaccination." There is no other way of feeding that protects a newborn baby like this.

After giving birth, it is natural that the mother and the baby do not separate, and this is enabled in maternity wards with a baby-friendly programs. This ensures the conditions for unlimited breastfeeding (i.e. breastfeeding as needed by the baby, day and night). If the first days are missed, successful breastfeeding is far more difficult and sometimes impossible.

Breastfeeding is more successful if the baby is immediately placed on the breast, immediately after giving birth, because she already knows that it is sucking. The baby should not be fed on any schedule, but when she wishes. In the first days after birth, a break between feedings should not be greater than three hours. The baby needs to suck until it is full. Then she will either to refuse the breast or go to sleep. Many infants, especially premature babies, prefer to doze during feedings.

In the first two weeks, a mother is creating her feeding habits. A baby who weighs more than three pounds during the first two weeks of life mother should wake up once in a day only if she sleeps more than four hours, and at night it is not necessary to wake up her at all. A baby lighter than three pounds should wake up for three hours.

First feeding: successes of the first week—a guarantee a month ahead

The first feeding of a baby is an exciting event, which must occur as soon as the baby is born. Do not despair, if you feel that the child can only suck for a short time. Be patient. Newborns do not need much milk, mothers need to get used to new sensations.

During this period, it is important that the baby is next to you; this will allow you to understand the baby and feed her when she needs milk. The baby may lie calm and calm down at the breast, without paying attention to your efforts to feed it. Report this to your doctor or nurse and try to find out the reason. In any case, try to empty the breast so that milk production does not stop. And do not torture yourself with your thoughts, wondering if everything is okay with a baby, whether you have enough milk and whether you can feed a child, whether your form of nipples is correct, etc. Just stay with your child alone (at least mentally) and try to find an understanding.

A mother's chest size does not have a significant effect on breastfeeding. Babies are equally well-fed by women with small or large breasts. The first few days of feeding a baby are better when the mother is lying down. This will allow her to relax, tune in to get positive emotions—which by itself stimulates the production of milk—and reduce tension in the mother's back muscles, which will prevent her from becoming tired. Gradually, as you get used to feeding your baby, it will become more comfortable, but it is important to adhere to some rules.

Before feeding, get into a comfortable position, as feeding may take up to an hour. Do not forget that the atmosphere during feeding should be calm, even if you feed the baby in an environment that is strange or dynamic.

If the breast is engorged, you make a warm compress. However, it is imperative that everything touches your chest in some way is sterile.

If you are more comfortable feeding while sitting, sit so that the back has a support. If you are sitting on a bed, put several pillows under your back, and position one knee to hold the baby up a little higher. Place one pillow under this knee, as this will take on the weight of the baby, and you will be more comfortable.

The baby will instinctually find a nipple a nipple, but it is helpful in the first month to touch the baby's cheek near the corner of her mouth with a nipple or fingertip. Before the baby feeds, express a few drops to "clean" the dairy strokes.

When feeding, the areola should be completely in the mouth of the child; if it is too large for this, then its upper edge should be over the baby's mouth, and the bottom should be completely in the oral cavity. This is very important for preventing nipple cracks. The unpleasant and even painful sensations caused by the wrong chest infiltration of the baby are the first symptoms that indicate the possibility of cracks.

Make sure the baby is able to breathe freely while feeding. The unique ability to suck and breathe simultaneously is characteristic only for children up to two-and-a-half to three years of age. Because of this, it is unlikely that the baby will naturally be able to breathe freely while feeding. You must take care to ensure she is breathing as freely as possible as she feeds.

Pay attention to the position of the child: her head should be higher than the rest of her body, her nose should be free, and her mouth should cover the entire nipple and areola. It is better if the baby is undressed and covered with a blanket, so that she can move constantly, touching her arms to her mother's breast and expressing emotions. This close contact is good for both of you.

Sometimes the baby can get tired and fall asleep before she finishes feeding. This happens when only a small amount of milk is expressed or very soon after childbirth, when she has not yet gained strength. To fix this, swipe your finger or nipple around the corner of a mouth. The baby will try to grab the nipple again and start sucking. It is advisable that during the feeding the baby receives milk only from one breast. If she does not get enough milk, allow her to feed from the second breast. After feeding, empty both breasts, preserving the milk just in case the next feeding does not produce enough milk and the baby is still hungry.

Do not allow the baby to suck the nipple while feeding; this is the main cause of breast inflammation and the appearance of cracks. If the baby is sucking, she child has to rhythmically squeeze her chest with gums, pressing on tanks with milk, located under the areola. When she just sucks, milk will struggle to flow and feeding may be painful. If your baby is just sucking, it is better to interrupt her feeding. Be careful not to damage the nipple: put your little finger in the corner of your baby's mouth and try to open the mouth. After that, give the baby your breast once again and try to prevent her from just sucking.

Duration of feeding can vary, but in most cases the child is fed for 15-20 minutes. Some children can feed for the first time for 40-50 minutes. Talk to your baby while feeding: talking to her is as needed as the milk. After feeding, hold the child upright, flattening her tummy gently. This allows the air that entered the stomach during feeding to come out, and the baby will not be bothered by cramps.

Signs of proper breastfeeding:

- The chin of the baby touches the mother's chest.
- The baby's mouth is wide open.
- The lower lip is twisted outward.
- The child takes more of the lower part of the areola.
- The baby's calves are rounded or spread on the mother's chest.
- The mother does not feel pain during feeding.

Some women may have difficulties in breastfeeding because of their retracted or flat nipples. However, the length and shape of the nipples are not significant. During feeding, the areola and nipples will take on the desired form in the cavity of the child's mouth. With frequent breastfeeding, the child gradually adapts.

Does the child have enough milk?

Practically every mother, at first, worries that her baby is not eating, especially when the baby cries so often. Of course, in addition to hunger there are other reasons for a baby to cry. Often, mom is concerned about the quality of breast milk: it seems that it does not have enough calories, especially when compared in appearance with cow's milk.

Often, for this reason, mothers who are quite capable of breastfeeding their baby think about "rescue" of artificial mixtures. It is very important not to be mistaken or to let worries lead you to a decision to feed the child with a mixture or completely transition to artificial feeding.

The main indicator of a sufficient amount of breast milk is how the baby gains weight. If you can not weigh her over the course of a month, focus on the amount of urination and excrement. If a baby urinates less than seven times a day and the urine has an intense yellow color, or if the urine is less frequent (once every two to three days), it is likely that she has not had enough milk.

Another the reliable benchmark is the amount of milk in the chest. If before each feeding you have swollen breasts, the child sucks actively and fully, and after feeding you have something to drain, then it is unlikely that the baby is restless due to malnutrition.

Is it necessary to squeeze milk after feeding?

As long as the milk production is established, it is necessary to squeeze out milk after feeding. If a child for some reason does not allow breastfeeding, squeezing allows the breast to adjust and maintain lactation. In this case, the milk is to be fed according to the feeding regimen of the child—after three hours or depending on the filling of the mammary gland.

It should be remembered that the main role in the "chipping of the chest" and the establishment of lactation belongs to the child herself—she actively sucks out the formed milk. That is why it is so important to feed the baby "on demand."

Later, when the feeding is established, the child will feel satiated and calm after feeding, and the stagnant phenomena in the breast will not disturb mom. The need for milk squeezing will surely disappear. Usually these difficulties end about two to three months after childbirth. You may need to squeeze milk a little longer, but once you get used to it, you will not feel any more labor or trouble with this procedure. Remember that chest emptying by squeezing stimulates the release of milk. Drain the milk residue from the breast from which you were feeding the baby.

How do you squeeze milk?

It would be great if you were taught to squeeze milk in the hospital, immediately after childbirth. This procedure is not as complicated as it may seem at first, and it can be done manually or with the help of a suction cup. Put the infant in a crib in a calm atmosphere while you try to squeeze out. For this you will only need a sterile vessel (if you intend to use this milk later) and clean hands.

Squeezing is done with two hands: the left should stroke the gland in the direction towards the nipple, and the right should squeeze the milk, pressing the thumb and forefinger on the areola. Try to to grab the whole area around the areola, allowing the chest will drain more intensely. You will not be able to squeeze the milk to the last drop, but try to maximize the amount of milk that is drained. If you need to drain as much milk as possible, take a warm shower or apply a pre-heated towel beforehand. The squeezing of the milk with a suction cup is not as tedious as the hands, but its effectiveness depends on the quality of the device.

What to do when the kid refuses the breast

This may happen when the mother is forced to interrupt her contact with the child, often when continuing education or going to work, and the child has to alternate between breastfeeding and using a bottle. It is easier to feed from a bottle, which is why the child may refuse to breastfeed when the mother is present.

There are several solutions to this situation.

First, try to feed the baby from a spoon or a small cup instead of a bottle; if this fails, make sure that the child's efforts during "eating" are the same when bottle and breastfeeding. To do this, you need to use a natural nipple on the bottle and change it in time.

If you have produced enough milk and the baby cries during breastfeeding only because of the desire to feed the easier way, try to insist on breastfeeding. With enough parenting, it is quite possible for the baby to learn to prefer breastfeeding over a bottle.

In the extreme case, you can feed with a bottle or cup filled with breast milk. Some mothers thus feed children up to eight or nine months. If you, after consulting a pediatrician, have come to the conclusion that you are not producing enough milk, then properly organize the feeding of the baby with a milk mixture, but do not remove breast milk from the baby's diet too quickly.

Do not hurry to feed with a mixture!

Make every effort to increase the amount of milk.

To do this you should:

- rest in the afternoon as much as you need to feel positive;
- forget for some time about cleaning and washing at home,
- and share the process of cooking with some relatives;
- pay special attention to your nutrition and lifestyle;
- increase the amount of feeding temporarily to 10-12 times a day;
- and put the baby on both breasts during each feeding, and after feeding
- try to fall asleep with her or just relax (if she does not have enough milk, she will wake up sooner than usual).

Sometimes you can also increase the amount of milk using mixtures of herbs and specially cooked drinks. Be sure to feed the baby at night to activate the production of a hormone (prolactin) that promotes the production of milk. If there is a need to breastfeed the baby, use a spoon with a small cup, but not a pacifier. In this case, children refuse to breastfeed much less often.

Chapter 3. Next Three to Four Months of Breastfeeding

Babies eat every three to four hours (8-12 times a day) in the first month. This is because they have a small stomach, and the milk production changes rapidly. However, that does not mean they do not get enough milk.

How do you know when the baby is hungry?

Look out for these signs of hunger: winding (turning her head to your hand when you touch her cheeks), penetrating the ears, sucking, putting your hands in her mouth, and of course crying (this is the last sign, and it is best to feed the baby before she starts to cry).

Do not feed the baby on a set schedule. Allow your baby to drink as much as she needs to, when she needs to.

Growth spurts usually occur at two weeks, six weeks, and three months. At these times, the baby will eat more, and it is likely that she will have disturbing dreams.

If you are planning to both breastfeed and to feed with a bottle, it is best to wait four to eight weeks before introducing a bottle, in order to avoid confusion.

Between two and four months, continue breastfeeding according to your baby's needs.

Breastfeed your baby eight times during 24 hours. Frequently breastfeeding will help you to produce more milk.

Three or four-month-old infants need six to eight servings per day (in 24 hours). Most infants wake up to feed one or two times a night. As for the frequency of breastfeeding, it is best to adjust to the baby and offer her breast milk whenever she cries or shows other signs of hunger. If breastfeeding is not possible or you have decided that you do not want to breastfeed, the appropriate replacement for the breast milk is a factory-adapted milk for babies.

A Breastfeeding Schedule

Mothers are advised that it is most important for babies to establish a rhythm.The most important thing to focus on and keep track of is how many times a day your baby feeds, in order to prevent confusion about whether or not your baby is hungry.

Most babies need to feed at least 8 to 12 times each day, but many parents believe this means that their baby needs to be fed every two to three hours. To keep track of feeding times, the mother should keep a journal of breastfeeding.

Babies love routine, because it allows them to feel safe in being able to predict what is going to happen next. This allows them to be relaxed.

An important part of the routine is sleep, and there is a lot of debate about whether the baby needs to woken up to be fed.

Babies that weigh 6 pounds 10 ounces or more during the first month of life should wake during the day only if they sleep more than four hours, and they do not need to be woken up at night at all.

Babies that are lighter than 6 pounds 10 ounces should be awake for three hours, and more often if feeding is needed in the day and night, until the baby weighs 6 pounds 10 ounces. In general, the number of feedings within 24 hours does not matter if the child is progressing well, but it should not be less than seven feedings per day in the first month.

For the first six months, the World Health Organization recommends that the baby be only breastfed, and be fed "on demand" (every time the baby is awake or nervous, the mother should offer her breast). Only after the sixth month, the baby needs to be introduced to solid food, and breastfeeding is still advised until the second year of life.

Your baby may be hungrier during one session than during another, and there is no cause for concern if your baby is sucking faster or slower. It is also normal if the baby sometimes sucks just on one breast and sometimes wants to cross to the other breast as well.

You should be breastfeeding with the first signs of hunger: if she's awake, sucking your hand, kicking the mouth or eyes, stretching, etc. To a baby, breastfeeding is a stimulator, and babies often need to be put on the mother's chest to feel her presence.

Chapter 4. Breastfeeding Diet Tips

Mother's milk is the perfect food for a baby's growth and development. To make the milk most useful, the mother should maintain a healthy diet.

If you breastfeed, your calorie intake should be higher than usual by about 300 calories. If you reduce your calorie intake, you can ruin your health, as your body will use nutrients its reserve nutrients to make milk. This can cause fatigue and reduce immune-supporting factors in milk, so the baby will be less resistant to colds and infections.

Worse still, you will not have enough milk. You can lose from 1 pound to 4 pounds 6 ounces of weight per month without compromising on milk production. Significant weight loss (more than 1 pound per week) is associated with the release of harmful substances (found in fatty tissue) into breast milk.

You will have the greatest caloric needs in the first four to six months, (i.e. at the stage when the baby is breastfed). To supplement your diet, you may add, for example, three carbohydrate servings, 3-4 ounces of meat or poultry, one serving of fruit or vegetables, and one additional serving of dairy products daily. When your baby starts eating healthy foods other than breast milk, these supplements to your diet can be abolished.

Useful for mom, useful for baby

A mother's diet should not include foods that are "supernatural" or. The nutrition of a breastfeeding woman is slightly different from her nutrition during pregnancy. While breastfeeding, the amount of fluid intake should be significantly increased. Under the condition of good lactation, the mother is almost always thirsty. However, the idea that drinking more fluids will lead to producing more breast milk is false. Usually, a mother's thirst corresponds with the amount of milk produced.

The amount of liquid consumed per day must be not less than two liters; in the hot season, a mother should drink more. It may be advisable to drink an extra glass of juice, milk, or tea (preferably green tea, consumed 20-30 minutes before feeding the baby). It is not recommended to consume products containing allergenic properties (e.g., citrus, chocolate, etc.) that contain a large number of essential oils, spices, and extracts. Even a small chocolate candy eaten by a mother can cause an allergic reaction in the baby. Fruits and vegetables are perfect snacks.

It is also important for mothers to control the intake of fat from food—fat should account for no more than 30% of daily caloric content. Vegetable-derived fats are better than animal fats. Since glucose is absorbed very quickly, do not consume a lot of sugar.

However, by limiting the number of sweets and sugary drinks you should not exclude them entirely: glucose is very necessary for your body. It quickly relieves fatigue, tension, and even bad moods. Additionally, total salt in food (preferably iodized) should be approximately one teaspoon a day. Cooking in steam, in a microwave oven, and baking will help reduce the amount of fat, butter, oil, salt, and sugar in a mother's diet, and it will also exclude many harmful extracts.

A mother's diet should include many vitamins, as the presence of these vitamins in breast milk is very important for the normal development of the child. Some vitamins can also stimulate milk production. They are found in large quantities in bananas, blueberries, mulberries, cherries, raspberries, and tea.

While you still do not know the gastronomic preferences of your child, it is better to refuse coffee while breastfeeding. As your child grows up, you may have the occasional cup of coffee and observe how it affects your child's behavior. If coffee does have a positive effect on your mood, it is likely that your good mood will in turn have a positive effect on the child.

Finally, it is best to refrain from consuming alcoholic beverages or using drugs while breastfeeding. If you do sometimes consume alcohol, the total amount of pure alcohol your drinks should not exceed 20 ml per day.

Basic Nutrition Guide

If you follow these instructions, you will have a high enough caloric intake and sufficient amount of high-quality milk for your baby:

— Eat when you're hungry.
— Take a glass of water or fresh milk whenever you breastfeed your baby.
— Maintain a balanced diet.
— Remember that breakfast gives "full gas" to your metabolic rate, burning calories faster than when you skip meals.
— Some cereals are the basis of meals (eat whole meal, brown, spinach) because they prevent constipation.

— Eat a variety of foods, as the variety of smells and tastes in your milk will help your baby more easily accept other foods.

— Fruits and vegetables are of particular importance because they contain necessary minerals and vitamins.

— It's important to maintain an adequate protein intake. Meat provides the right amount of protein in your diet—which is about 3 ounces a day for a breastfeeding mother. Red meat also provides vitamin B6, iron, and zinc. In addition, protein can be found in milk, eggs, fish, or poultry.

— Avoid sweet and greasy foods, as well as sweet juices.

— Avoid nuts in general.

— Drink before you become thirsty, because thirst is an early dehydration symptom (drink enough that your urine is light yellow in color). Consume healthy drinks, especially during warm summer months. Healthy drinks include water, natural juices from fruits and vegetables, milk, soup.

— Increase Vitamin B intake to stimulate milk production. Vitamin B is found in yeast and grains. The lack of this vitamin can upset the child.

— Drugs, including prescribed medications, pass into breast milk. If you have to take them, be sure they will not harm the baby.

— Quit smoking and drinking alcohol.

— Keep in mind that caffeine is a strong stimulant, and it can cause gas in babies.

— Certain foods with a strong scent (for example, onions, broccoli, cabbage, cauliflower, or spices) can make your skin unpleasant and cause some babies to become upset. If that happens, take a break in those foods.

— Calcium is very important, and recent research has shown that calcium and other components of dairy products suppress hormones that aid fat accumulation.Some babies do not tolerate cow's milk protein, which may have been your main source of calcium. For other sources of calcium, try broccoli, cabbage, orange juice, cereals, pumpkin, and salmon.

Chapter 5. Lactation Tips

At the very beginning of life, babies spend almost the whole day sleeping and eating. Nature has provided you with the necessary equipment and skills to nursing the baby, but it will not hurt to acquire some additional knowledge.

Care of breasts before and after feeding:

- Before breastfeeding, wash hands thoroughly with warm water and soap.
- Pre-breastfeed a few drops of milk from the breast and then spread across the nipples and areolas to help the baby smell and taste the milk.
- If your breasts are swollen and full of milk, it is recommended that you massage the breast before breastfeeding in order to soften the areola and prepare for successful breastfeeding.

- If the breasts remain full after breastfeeding, excess breast milk should be removed from the breast.
- After expelling a few drops of milk, spread the milk around the nipples and areolas again and let them air dry.
- The breast should be exposed to the air regularly.

How to Massage Your Breasts?

In the case of an overproduction of milk and swollen breasts, it is necessary to lightly massage the breasts, following these steps:

- Before the massage, place a warm compress on the breast, or gently massage it with warm water.
- Start at the base of the shoulder, using only your fingertips.
- Move in light, concentric circular movements across the entire breast.

- Leaning forward may help expel breast milk, taking advantage of gravity in the massage.
- Place cold compresses on the breast.
- Take hot baths and showers allowing the warm water to cover the shoulder and breast.

What do you do if the infant falls asleep during feedings?

Experts say that the baby does not need to wake up during the feeding, as long as she is actively sucking and it takes no more than three hours for her to take a meal. The exceptions are babies born with low birth weight, sleepy babies who have elevated levels of bilirubin, and a group of babies that we call "lazy" and sick babies. These babies should be woken up by gently massaging the soles of the feet, legs, or back.

When should a mother stop breastfeeding?

- Every time the baby has not properly caught the breast

- If the act is painful
- When the baby takes a long break in breastfeeding
- If the baby gets upset or irritable

How should mother's milk be stored?

You may find yourself in a situation where you have many hours away from home other otherwise unable breastfeed your baby. For example, you may need to go to the hospital due to disease, you made need to leave to go to work, or you need a break from breastfeeding because of an infection in the breast. What do you do then, and how do you make sure your baby does not reject your breast later?

You can preserve your milk to be used when needed. The maintenance of the mother's milk begins with a suction process, either by hand or by a pump (hand or electric).

The mother's milk can be stored in a sterile sealed container at room temperature of 18-20° C for about three to four hours. It may also be stored in the refrigerator at 4-5° C for about 24 hours (up to 72 hours maximum). It can also be frozen at -18--20° C for up to four months.

Note: Never heat the milk for breastfeeding directly on a pot or in a microwave oven.

A mother's milk should never be shaken, but stirred in circular movements instead.

Chapter 6. Weaning: When to Start Weaning, How to Quit Breastfeeding, and Introducing Solid Food

The best way to stop breastfeeding is to do so gradually. Every three to four days, stop breastfeeding. Repeating this will give a strong signal and will give your breast enough time to reduce milk production. In this way, the mother and the child can find a way to compensate for the moments of closeness they have had during the time of breastfeeding.

Planned breastfeeding refers to the when a mother plans to stop breastfeeding completely regardless of whether the baby is ready for it. A sudden break in breastfeeding is equally difficult for both mother and baby. It is only used when it is necessary and the only option.

If the mother feels her breasts are quickly filled with milk after breastfeeding, it is likely that she is trying to stop breastfeeding too quickly and needs to slow down.

If the mother decides that she wants to continue breastfeeding, it is of course still possible. There is no reason to stop breastfeeding because the milk in the breast cannot go bad.

How long should you breastfeed?

- o Mom and baby should decide how long breastfeeding will last.

- In the first six months, it is ideal for the baby to only consume mother's milk.
- If the mother does not have enough milk for all meals, it is important to have as much baby's formula as needed.
- Avoid breastfeeding breaks, because breast milk protects against stomach infections.
- Don't plan to quit breastfeeding at the moment you want to return to work.

In most breastfeeding women, lactation gradually fades until the end of the first year of the baby's life. At this point, one evening feeding is maintained, which is later replaced by cow's milk, especially if the mother is not producing enough milk. At one year old, the baby is at an age when she can satisfy the need for food and comfort from other sources than her mother's breast.

Nowadays, more and more gynecologists and pediatricians insist that breastfeeding should be continued up to two to three years after childbirth, or even more. In my opinion, the most optimal situation is the preservation of breastfeeding up to one to one-and-a-half years. If the mother is producing milk, then cow's milk is unlikely to be better, but it is not necessary to turn the chest into a means of calming the baby. An exception, of course, is the situation when the baby is ill. In this case, the focus is on helping the baby recover, and breast milk is incredibly beneficial in this case.

Observations on children that were breastfed for a long time did not reveal any differences in their state of health from those that were breastfed for a shorter amount of time. At the same time, most mothers point out that breastfeeding later on becomes a peculiar ritual or habit. If you breastfeed your baby before bed, and she does not wake up at night and does not mention it in the day, then there is no problem with breastfeeding for longer. But if, after one year, the child does not require a breast not because of hunger, but because of a lesser sense of discomfort or as a means of resolving conflict, it is not necessary to breastfeed for more than 18 months.

Note: To wean the baby from the breast in the summer or during the illness is not recommended.

How do you stop breastfeeding?

It is important to stop breastfeeding properly and finding the right moment, which will be when you and your baby are ready. Your baby will show by itself and make it clear to you that she is ready to stop breastfeeding. Do not miss this moment.

- ✓ Gradually reduce the number of feedings. First, reduce daily feedings, following by morning and end of the evening feedings.

✓ Support your child in the transition by focusing on pampering, transitional object (doll tranquilizer), and actively spending free time with the baby. This helps the baby overcome the transition from the secure bond that develops between mothers and babies.

For three decades, it was the "rule—that the mother should give up breastfeeding for four months, six is enough, and over eight has no need." This proved to be a false teaching because of the huge number of serious scientific and clinical research that have shown that the benefits of breastfeeding are invaluable, and that the effects on a child's development are better when the mother breastfeeds longer.

For a long time, mothers were encouraged to continue breastfeeding during the second year of the baby's life—of course, with respect to the principle of healthy nutrition and the fact that milk is NOT the main food at this age. The variety of non-lactic diet is "a pillar" of health, but it also goes well with the mother's milk, which provides a number of benefits for the child.

Babies after a full year do not need more than 400 ml of milk a day. Yogurt is also included in a babies diet, so breastfeeding one to two times per day is quite enough in this period.

After the second birthday, the vast majority of children are ready for cow's milk and products (provided that there are no allergic reactions or intolerance), and "psychological" attachment to the mother becomes a key reason for continuing to breastfeed.

The child is thus soothed and "enjoys" breastfeeding, but it can become a burden to the mother. This can also make the child frustrated, she may not be breastfed when she wants. The mother is still of major importance for the baby, but in the third year of child's life, breastfeeding is NOT the main way to deepen this relationship.

It is advisable to continue breastfeeding until springtime, to allow your child to strengthen her immune system during the cold months, which are so full of viruses and other attacks on the immune system. Once spring arrives, it is wise to stop breastfeeding.

The natural approach is the best—the feedings should gradually be shortened, then cut, and then stopped. If "excess" milk remains, it can be frozen, but after the final decision to stop breastfeeding there is NO return!

If the child returns to breastfeeding, "on the breast" milk will again begin to be produced, because the child's sucking will stimulate lactation. Therefore, when a decision is made, a mother should stick to it, even though the child will be in a state of denial initially.

Chapter 7. How to Prevent Nipple Pain and How to Treat Sore Nipples

If your child is properly latched on and sucking efficiently, you should not feel pain. If you think your baby is not sucking well, disconnect the vacuum between the child's mouth and your breast by putting your finger in the corner of the child's mouth and gently pulling the nipple. After that, try again to properly place the baby on the breast. Improper sucking will only worsen the pain in your nipples and lead to a bad breastfeeding technique that is difficult to correct.

If in the meantime both you and your child are upset, stop slightly, calm down, and then continue. The child will eventually learn to properly breastfeed.

If the pain in the nipples continues, check the following:

- Is the child's mouth wide open when it accepts the breast so that the nipple is deep in the mouth?
- Are the child's lips curled out? When children hold their lips together around the nipple and areola, their sucking can cause pain.
- If you lightly pull the child's lower lip during feeding, can you see her tongue between the lower lip and the nipple? If you do not see it, the child may suck it with your nipple. In this case, remove the baby from the breast and start over again. Make sure the child's mouth is very open, whether the tongue is below the nipple or above the gums.

In the first days after birth, the breasts swell due to milk that goes "tide." This phenomenon can be alleviated by frequent exposure. When your breasts are full and firm, it can be difficult for a child to accept them. Put on warm compresses and massage your breasts gently. Try to squeeze some milk to soften the area around the areola before breastfeeding.

Ice can soothe and soften nipples of all sizes. Crush the ice, put it in a wet towel, and place it on the nipple for a short time before washing. The ice can also numb the painful nipple so that the pain that occurs at the start of the breastfeeding session is easier to bear.

Flat or inverted nipples: There are many ways of treating these nipples, but studies are not in agreement about their effectiveness. If you have flat or wound nipples, you will need expert help on the correct placement of babies on the breast. And do not forget—the child will not suck from the nipple itself.

You can manually, regularly express some milk to stimulate lactation before putting the child on the painful breast. Or, if only one nipple is painful, start to breastfeed on the other breast until the pain subsides. Then, switch your baby to the painful breast. Be very careful and persistent in maintaining the correct position.

If your nipples are very painful, you can reduce pain by change positions during the feeding. As you change positions, pressure will be put on different parts of the nipples. Whatever position you choose, always make sure that the baby is close enough to the breast so that it can be properly caught. The mouth must be "full of the breast."

Most newborns breastfeed 10-12 times in the course of 24 hours. Such frequent feedings do not contribute to pain in the nipples. A child who is not hungry will nourish more than a hungry baby, and she will be much more patient if you have to remove her from the breast several times to correct the position.

Chapter 8. Quick Tips and Hints for Breastfeeding Mothers

When and how often should the baby breastfeed?

Breastfeed the baby always when she is hungry. The baby, therefore, is breastfed as needed, and within a few days, the amount of milk produced adjusts to the baby's needs. If your baby's appetite increases, she will want to drink more often. This will stimulate milk production and your milk quantity will adapt to the "increased demand." If your breast produces more milk, the gap between feeding will automatically increase again.

Is my baby getting enough milk?

The amount your baby drinks can vary greatly from meal to meal, as well as from day to day.

One indication that you have enough milk is that your baby has four to five full nappies per day. Additionally, you can place your baby on a scale weekly and see how much weight she has gained.

Breast care during breastfeeding

To ensure healthy breastfeeding, it is important to take care of your breasts properly. They are, after all, the main source of food for your baby. For proper breast care, do the following:

Wear a comfortable bra for nursing mothers during the day and night.

✓ After each feeding, wash breast exclusively with water, then carefully wipe them.

✓ Avoid soap and shower gels that contain alcohol or have a strong odor because they can dry your breast skin, which can then lead to cracks and pain.

Although you will probably want to lose weight as soon as you give birth, this is not the time to start a diet. Your body needs extra calories to produce enough milk. The best advice is that you have a well-balanced diet. This will allow you to provide your baby with the most nutritious breast milk.

Relax and Breathe

This is more important for you than for the baby.

In the beginning, you may be sitting in uncomfortable positions, with wrinkled shoulders and crooked posture, which will make your spine more strained. Practice gently breathing, relax your shoulders, and fall into the chair as much as you can. It is important for you to enjoy breastfeeding as your baby enjoys it.

Each breastfeed lasts for 15-25 minutes, depending on the nature and strength of the baby. When one breast is completely empty, you should offer your baby another. The next breastfeeding session begins with the breast that was last in the previous session.

There are very few reasons why a mother may not be able to breastfeed her baby, either because of her health or the baby's health.

Manual and Electric Breast Pumps

The pumps are basically designed to imitate the baby's movements when sucking. This means that when you put the pump on your chest, the kicking starts with a quick press, and then the number of lever pressures slows down over time, and the intervals between the two lever presses become longer.

Studies have shown that the baby's sucking creates a vacuum and pulls under a pressure of 0.29 bar, and this pressure lasts for one second on average. Most good pumps, either electric or manual, are imitating this way of pumping milk.

Depending on your needs, you can buy electrical or manual. The electric one is better, but it is also more expensive. Now you can also buy sterilizer pumps. However, if you are breastfeeding, and the pump will come to you as an additional help, then it is okay to choose a manual one.

For women with extremely large breasts, it is not possible to be pumped out with a manual pump, because you usually have to hold one breast with one hand while holding the other breast with the other hand. Depending on where your nipples are placed, the easier it is to use a manual pump. If it is low—

that is, if you have viscous breasts—there is no problem with using it manually.

Before purchasing and selecting a pump, answer the following questions:

- How often will you use the pump?

- What size are your breasts?

- Where are your nipples set?

You can ask and get help from your doctor or midwife at any point.

Breastfeeding twins

The mother of twins is lucky because she has too breast, isn't she? Yes, twin breastfeeding is quite possible and feasible, despite some bad stories that suggest it is impossible to breastfeed two children at once. The mothers of triplets can also breastfeed their children, but they will need great support.

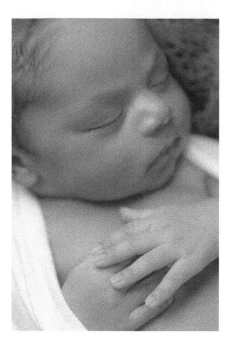

Enjoy!

Do not make the decision to stop breastfeeding fast, for whatever reason. Always consult your pediatrician or your physician beforehand.

Enjoy your love and closeness with your baby, from giving birth to breastfeeding, and do not forget to share those moments with your partner.

Some Books You May Find Interesting

Use these proven 3 days method to free your boy from dirty diapers!

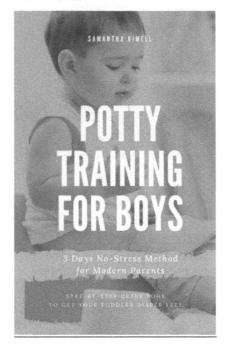

There are numerous potty training strategies, however, it is important to choose the right one for your kid. We look at a few of the most proficient methods to potty train a boy in book "Potty Training for Boys in 3 Days".

You`ll learn proven plan with clear steps to get your baby diaper-free without stress and tears. "Potty Training for Boys" in 3 days is your key to success in this important period of your`s family life.

This book covers everything you need to know and to do step-by-step. Potty Training in 3 Days is your key to forget about diapers for good.

Here Is A Preview Of What You'll Learn:

- How to prepare your child and make training a lot easier.

- The Clear Step-by-Step 3-Day Plan for every your action during and after potty training.

- If nothing helps (step-by-step plan based on a real story).

- Useful equipment for successful potty training for boys.

- Solutions for nighttime and naptime.

- Dealing with accidents.

+FREE BONUS Chapter. 41 Quick Tips and Solutions for Modern Parents for Successful Potty Training.

So make your Potty Training simple!

Proven Methods to Teach Your Baby to Sleep Through the Night. Simple and Healthy Solutions for Kids from Birth to 3 Years.

I wrote this book, "Baby Sleep Training: A Parent's Guide to Surviving and Overcoming Sleepless Nights," with new parents and parents-to-be in mind. I want to help you get over the hurdles of putting your little one to sleep and getting some shut-eye yourself.

As there is no single sleep solution that will fit all children, I will provide you with research-proven, parent-approved techniques so you can find the perfect approach that works for your little bundle of joy.

Here Is A Preview Of What You'll Learn:

- Baby Sleep Patterns (from 0 to 36 months)
- Establishing Healthy Sleep Habits
- 3 Most Effective Sleep Training Methods
- A Step-by-Step Guide to Successful Sleep Training
- The Dos and Don'ts of Sleep Training
- Coping with Sleepless Nights
- Coaching Babies to Sleep Based on Age

Sleep is more than just getting rest, it has the power to heal and does incredible things for the body and mind. And this book outlines the best techniques that ensure healthy sleep for every age.

Indispensable guide for improving your child's behavior!

I am not a bad parent, my child is not stubborn —
this has been my mantra for years, especially when
my youngest child, Sophia, entered her toddler
years.

Sophia wanted to learn things in her own way and
would do anything in her power to get what she likes
or prove that she was right. If her attention was
called because of a misbehavior, she would go on
into a meltdown.

You are probably going through the same scenario with your kid. Downloading this book may be your cry for help, and you desperately want to understand how you can deal with your "difficult" child.

The reason why I wrote this book is to help parents, such as yourself, to learn how they could deal with their spirited child and make them realize what nurturing and sensitive parenting can do to turn a "problematic" kid into a terrific teen or adult.

I share this book with you not only as a parent of a spirited child but also as a professional with years of experience working with kids with different personalities.

Here Is A Preview Of What You'll Learn:

- The 5 most effective parenting styles.
- Triggers that set your child off.
- Dealing with tantrums of the spirited child.
- 6 easy ways to bring out the best in your child.
- How to set limits and how to eliminate conflicts.

How to Communicate to Prevent Conflicts and Raise a Happy Child!

As a parent, can you honestly say that your little kids are really listening to you when you speak to them?

If so, then you can proudly claim having built a trustworthy relationship with them! Then, it's peanuts for you to engage their cooperation, set limits, and prevent conflicts in almost all aspects of their life for now...

As children grow, changes occur. Hey, it's hard being a little child, and similarly, it's tough being an adult who's in charge of that little growing kid. Life is a never-ending growing and changing. To cope with all of these, we need to learn.

I share this book with you not only as a parent, but also as a professional with years of experience working with kids with different personalities.

Here Is A Preview Of What You'll Learn:

- Building a Trustworthy Relationship.
- Helping with your Child's Negative Feelings.
- How to engage your Child's Willing Cooperation.
- Setting Limits and Rules.
- Punishment Alternatives.
- Resolving Family Conflicts in a Positive Manner.
- How to Prevent and Deal with Tantrums and Your Kid Being Stubborn.

Personally, I believe that parenting is the ultimate purpose of one's life. It is a choice you make, a challenge, the cross carried by some people, but a source of joy and fulfillment for many. How we tackle this task somehow defines who we are and the future of humanity...

Toddler Discipline: The Essential Guide to Positive Parenting

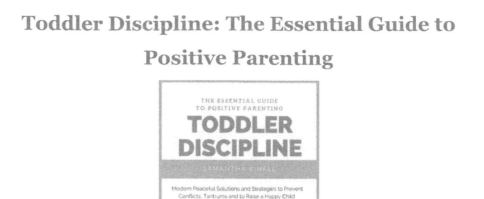

We will discuss the most effective strategies and solutions how to deal with behavioral problems, prevent tantrums and save the child's trust and love in this book.

You will learn how to understand, listen and discipline your child with the help of psychology and the best psychologist instrument in the world — your heart.

This book is the key to happy relationships, communication, and development of your child in a positive way. Apply these strategies and tips in practice and enjoy this period of a child's life without stress, tears, and tantrums for sure.

CPSIA information can be obtained
at www.ICGtesting.com
Printed in the USA
LVHW032050020120
642357LV00002B/234

9 781726 699754